# Eye Candy Quilts

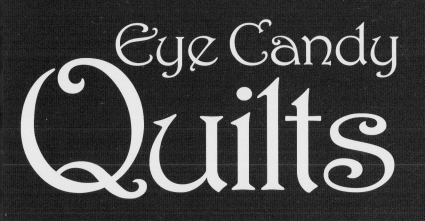

Super-fast fun
with beads, baubles,
buttons, and more!

# MELODY CRUST

with HEATHER OSTERMAN

*Breckling Press*

Library of Congress Cataloging-in-Publication Data

Crust, Melody.
Eye candy quilts : Super-fast fun with beads, baubles, buttons, and more! / Melody Crust with Heather Osterman.
p. cm.
ISBN 978-1-933308-25-8
1. Fancy work. 2. Quilting. 3. Miniature quilts. I. Osterman,
Heather. II. Title.

TT750.C947 2010
746.46--dc22

2009038298
This book was set in Stemple Schneidler and Harrington by High Tide Design
Editorial and production direction by Anne Knudsen
Art direction by Anne Knudsen
Design and production High Tide Design
Photography by Charles Crust

Published by Breckling Press
283 Michigan Ave.,
Elmhurst IL 60126 USA

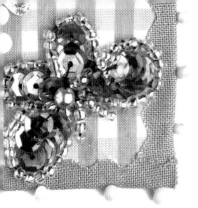

# Contents

# Dedication

For Marion R. Heath, eye candy then, now, and always

# Welcome to Eye Candy Quilts!

It's a busy world. So busy, that quilters and crafters ask for one type of project more often than any other: You want something that is fast and fun! The result, though, has to be absolutely beautiful.

This book was developed with our need for instant beauty in mind. These gorgeous mini-quilts are so much fun to make, they should be declared illegal! Many of them, like the quilt opposite, measure just 2½" x 3". Since they are small, you can finish one in practically no time. The wonderful variety of embellishments, from beads, buttons, and bows, to silk flowers, trims and countless other little fancies will win your work instant admiration. Their size makes them a snap to display, making them quick, easy gifts anyone will treasure.

Another huge attraction of Eye Candy Quilts is that they are a great way to try out new embellishing techniques, without taking too much time or expense. If you are like most quilters, you already have a stash of treasures just waiting a project to come along and claim them. And if you rummage through and don't find exactly what you need, then it's time to shop! Not only can you hunt for fabrics, but beads, buttons, and trims, too.

Enjoy every part of the process, from the shopping to the final creation, and you will truly experience the fun of Eye Candy Quilts. Pretty soon, you'll love them as much as we do!

*Melody Crust*
*Heather Osterman*

OPPOSITE: This stunning little quilt showcases everything we love about *Eye Candy Quilts*. It measures just 2½"x 3½". The red hand-painted fabric is the base, livened by an odd number of different colors and sizes of buttons. The dangles in the button centers add dimension and shine. The picot edge brings both the sparkle and 3-D design elements all the way to the edge.

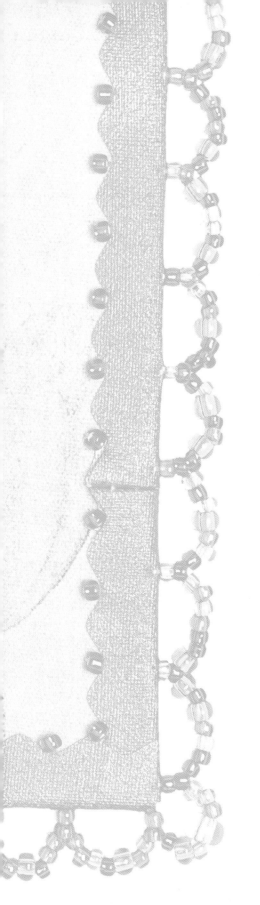

# Ready, Set, Go!

I can't imagine a faster, easier or more relaxing project than making an Eye Candy Quilt. They are so small that beginning one never has to be the least bit intimidating. You get to spend an hour or so doing something you enjoy, and in the end you will have a very pretty finished project to show for it.

OPPOSITE: This scalloped bead border perfectly frames fabric printed using my own computer. Like the flowers, the border is elegant in its simplicity, and draws its colors from the picture. 3" x 3½"

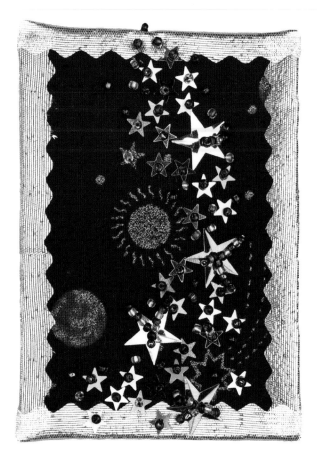

The fabric itself inspired the notion of creating my own Milky Way. The shiny star sequins attached with beads and dangles really livened up this night sky. A binding cut with a decorative-edge rotary cutter made a fast, easy and attractive binding. 2½" x 3½"

Eye Candy Quilts just invite innovation. Making them is pure playtime! Remember, when you are making one of these little beauties, it is not the same as making a once-in-lifetime king-sized quilt—no huge investment in time and money factors in here. This does not mean you should ignore good design principles when making your Eye Candy Quilt. It *does* mean, however, that you don't have to make all those important design decisions upfront; instead, an Eye Candy Quilt lets you make decisions as you go along, with the freedom to change plans as you progress. Once you begin, you'll realize how liberating this is, as you free yourself from making all your design decisions at the beginning of each project.

When starting an Eye Candy Quilt, I use a technique I think of as the "one-decision-at-a-time" method. Quite simply, I make a decision, commit to it (that is, sew it), take a look to see what I like about it, then either build on what I have or change direction.

All the little quilts in this book were created by making one decision at a time. In other words, I made a choice on fabric or an embellishment, sewed it, and then looked to see what it needed next. The designs grew in front of my eyes until each one felt complete to me. Nearly every Eye Candy Quilt created this way has been a delight and every single one has expanded my creative horizons by allowing me to explore design ideas and techniques I might never have tried on a full-sized quilt. Because Eye Candy Quilts are small, easy, and fast to make, experimentation is richly rewarded with one design discovery after another. Once you allow your ideas to blossom freely, your mind and fingers will fly as you try to keep up with them all.

Eye Candy Quilts are all about embellishing. You can use virtually anything at all, from simple beads to strange and wonderful found objects. As you read this book, and as you find out about the huge variety of embellishments available for your use, look carefully at the photographs. Each one features different materials, and the captions explain how they are used. Keep an open mind as you search for new embellishments—a wonderful world of discovery awaits you.

# Constructing an Eye Candy Quilt

Since the key characteristic of an Eye Candy Quilt is embellishment, these little quilts are constructed in a different sequence than their full-size cousins. With a traditional quilt the order of tasks is as follows: piece, appliqué or fuse the quilt top, embellish, then layer, quilt, and bind. With Eye Candy Quilts, embellishment moves to the very last step of the process. First you will make the quilt top, then layer, quilt, and bind it. This way, all your stitching or fusing is completely done before you pick up your first three-dimensional embellishment. The big advantage is that you will never have to stitch around or quilt through embellishments, allowing you much more freedom—and fun.

The first step, then, in creating an Eye Candy Quilt is to make what I call an "eye candy blank." Quite simply, this is a mini-quilt with the quilt top, backing, and binding already completed at the very beginning of the project. It is a ready-made blank canvas. I make several "eye candy blanks" at a time, so that they are ready and waiting for me when I want to try out a new embellishment technique. Sometimes, I quilt the blank to hold the layers together, but often I just leave it unquilted. I find that once I have attached beads, ribbons, lace, and more during the embellishment process, the layers hold together just fine without quilting. Also, since the binding is already in place, it's easy to embellish right over it, anchoring your binding as you go.

An Eye Candy Quilt can be any size you like. Small ones (3½" x 2½") are very quick to make. You may want to start with one of these. Larger Eye Candy Quilts give you room to "say" more. Let your creative mood be your guide – you needn't limit yourself to making just one particular size. Keep in mind that they look best when in proper proportion, length to width. If in doubt, consider the standard sizes that professional photographers use, such as 3" x 5", 5" x 7", or 8" x 10". These proportions work beautifully. If you are a beginner, you may want to avoid squares because it can be difficult to balance the overall design.

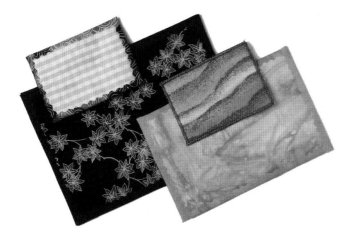

A collection of different sizes of eye candy blanks:  2½"x 3½", 4"x 6" and 5"x 7". Three are bound with pinked-edged fused bindings. The one in front has a simple thread binding done with a zigzag machine stitch.

100 percent polyester background fabric adds sheen and a nice woven texture. The shiny, faceted beads are circled with ribbon collars and more ribbon was added by "scrunching and bunching" it using the sharp point of a needle, before securing it with a variety of additional beads. 2½" x 3½"

# Making Eye Candy Blanks

For me, a good deal of the fun of Eye Candy Quilts is in the fast, free-wheeling, no-risk embellishing. Investing an evening making up numerous eye candy blanks assembly-line fashion is a quick and easy way to ensure you will have plenty of blank canvases to work with when the embellishing urge takes over. And believe me, it will! Here is how to make an eye candy blank in four easy steps.

**1** Cut the front, back, batting, and fusible web to the intended finished size.

**2** Adhere the fusible web to the back of the top fabric. Make lining everything up for fusing easier by adding a couple of small pieces of fusible in between the back and the batting.

**3** Layer in this order: Back (wrong side up); batting; and top (right side up). Press both sides with an iron.

**4** Choose a binding and sew it on (see page 9).

With a stack of colorful blanks at hand, you are ready to start embellishing, using any of the methods explained later in this book.

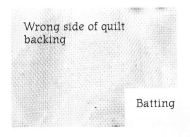

Wrong side of quilt backing

Batting

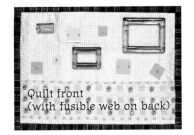

Quilt front (with fusible web on back)

Order of assembly (facing up): Wrong side of backing fabric, batting, and right side of front fabric.

## Quilt Backing

I like to make and label the backs all at one time using treated fabric in my ink jet printer. Once the words say just the right thing (and the spelling has been double-checked!), put the fabric through the printer. It's more efficient to print as many backs as possible on a single piece of treated fabric at one time. These treated-for-printing fabrics are usually white. Since I prefer colored fabrics, I paint on the white with textile paint mixed with 25 percent water and allow them to dry thoroughly before running them through the printer. Don't worry if your painted fabric looks a bit messy – just let it dry, iron it flat, and you are all set to follow the manufacturer's directions for printing.

When making larger Eye Candy Quilts, I often piece the back, using the label as part of the backing fabric.

I can't stress enough that it's important to claim your work! This is art and people want to know who the artist is. These backs were all made using my computer printer on fabric prepared for printing.

# Binding Eye Candy Quilts

Select your binding fabric. If you want your embellishments to really stand out, consider choosing a binding that matches the color of your background. If, on the other hand, you want to take this opportunity to utilize the binding as another decorative feature, make a bold color choice or try using a piece of ribbon or other trim.

There are a number of ways to bind these little quilts. You can fuse, make a thread binding or pipe the edges on your machine. You could even make a fabric frame. Choose the one that best suits your needs or your mood.

## Fused Binding

**1** Select a binding fabric, something that compliments your front fabric or potential embellishment choices.

**2** Cut fabric and fusible web about 3" wide and ½" longer than the longest side of your quilt. Remove the paper backing from one side, then fuse together into one piece.

**3** Rotary cut four strips. I allow for these bindings to be cut at about ⅝" wide. (Small quilts look better with narrow bindings.) Use a decorative cutter for extra interest. Fold in half lengthwise and finger press. Since Steam-A-Seam 2 Lite fusible web comes with paper on both sides, remove the second part of the paper backing.

**4** Fuse the binding to the short sides of the quilt and trim the ends. Repeat for the long sides. When trimming, be careful not to cut the short-side binding pieces.

Note that it's much easier to handle fusible web in slightly larger pieces—who in their right mind is going to want to try to fuse a stack of ⅝" strips when it isn't necessary? Cutting the fabric and fusing in larger pieces is a real time- and frustration-saver. For example, if your quilt is going to have a finished size of 5" x 7", you might want to cut the binding fabric and fusible 7½" (the length of the longest side plus an extra ½") x 3" (four sides at ⅝" wide each). After fusing, cut the

I keep leftover bits of fusible binding. These are all ready to be used as embellishments on future Eye Candy Quilts.

**Tip** *I use a double-stick fusible web (my favorite is Steam-A-Seam 2 Lite) to hold the layers together. I find it preferable to put the fusible web next to the front fabric. This way it provides extra support to hold what often becomes a lot of weight from beads and other embellishments.*

large piece into the $5/8''$ strips you need. If you like, you could make this larger piece of fused binding two or three times as large as this in either direction and then cut it into the strips you need. That way, you will have enough pre-made binding left over to bind the next mini-quilt or two.

Notice the lavender leftover binding bits that were used here along with some jewelry beads purchased at the craft store to make this clematis-inspired trellis Eye Candy Quilt. 5" x 7"

Buttons, ribbons and a variety of beads all contribute to this Eye Candy. The vertical lines are deliberately at a slight slant to create the feeling of lively movement, which matches the playfulness of the design. The colorful buttonhole stitching adds texture and helps hold the binding in place. 2½" x 3½"

# Fused Frame Binding

Notice that the quilt shown opposite isn't really bound, but framed, giving it a different look than a separate fused binding. This may well suit your overall design better. To make a fused frame binding, follow these steps.

**1** Cut the fusible web, backing, and frame fabrics 1" larger than the quilt's finished size.

**2** Fuse the frame and backing fabrics together.

**3** Before you embellish, stack the frame (right side up), fusible web, batting, more fusible web, Eye Candy Quilt (right side up) and fuse everything together.

**4** There will be a raw edge showing around your mini-quilt that you will probably want to cover with beads, decorative trim or thread as you embellish it.

You can machine stitch trim to cover the raw edges when attaching your Eye Candy Quilt to a fusible frame.

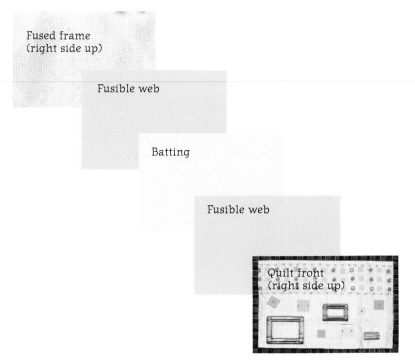

Placement of an Eye Candy Quilt within a fused frame

An Eye Candy Quilt can be framed rather than bound. This polka dot frame consists of two pieces of fabric fused together with a firm fusible web which allows it to stand on edge for easy display. 4½" x 5½".

**ABOVE:** If an edging trim doesn't fit your overall design, another option is to stitch the edges of the center section to the fused frame. Here, I used a very wide zigzag in an unobtrusive color and caught the ends of the ribbon in the stitching because I liked the look. 5" x 3"

**OPPOSITE:** The binding and yellow accent pieces are all machine stitched. The silver shapes were purchased jewelry pieces that I just loved. The orange jewels that fit the centers were in my stash, but didn't quite fit the "buds" or smaller rings, so I utilized a few smaller seed beads for them. I took another look and decided that everything needed to look more important, so I added the orange seed beads to the outside edges of the flowers. This is a slightly larger Eye Candy Quilt with a lot of lively action to it. The two-colored binding and piping was not only fast but serves to effectively frame the quilt. 10" x 12"

## Thread Binding

With this method, the thread is the binding. Pick a thread that either contrasts or matches the quilt; the choice is up to you. Thread binding is done on the sewing machine with a zigzag stitch. Use a stabilizer to make the stitching even. I prefer to use two layers of a lightweight tear-away. After sewing, remove one piece of the stabilizer at a time to help prevent accidentally distorting your stitches by pulling too hard. Test a sample to find the length and width of stitch that works best. I often add a piece of yarn or other round trim to help fill in the thread.

Using color-blocked thread is a simple but effective way to bind a quilt. The richly textured background fabric suggested this rather tailored-looking finished edge. 2½" x 3½"

# Super Fast Binding and Piping

Bindings and piping are a snap with this no-fail, completely machine-stitched method, making it a really fast and easy binding choice for larger Eye Candy Quilts. This is a simple but very effective twist on a traditional binding.

**1** Cut two sets of strips: Piping—1¼" wide; binding—1" wide.

**2** Sew the long sides together using a ¼" seam allowance.

**3** Press the seam to the binding. Use spray starch for a crisp, easy-to-handle binding.

**4** Fold in half lengthwise and press.

**5** Align the right side of the binding fabric against the back of the quilt and sew with a scant ¼" seam.

**6** Fold to the front, using a thread to match the piping. Top stitch in the ditch.

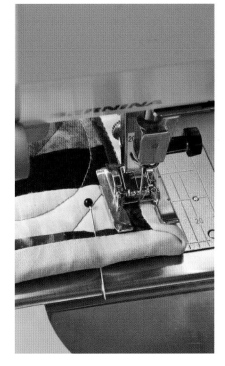

The binding is folded sharply over a ruler.

To make stitching around the corners easier, stop a couple of inches before you reach the corner, fold the bottom binding up, then fold the side binding over. The side you are stitching goes on top of the side you are going to stitch next, so there is no "pocket" to catch your presser foot, which also makes a prettier corner.

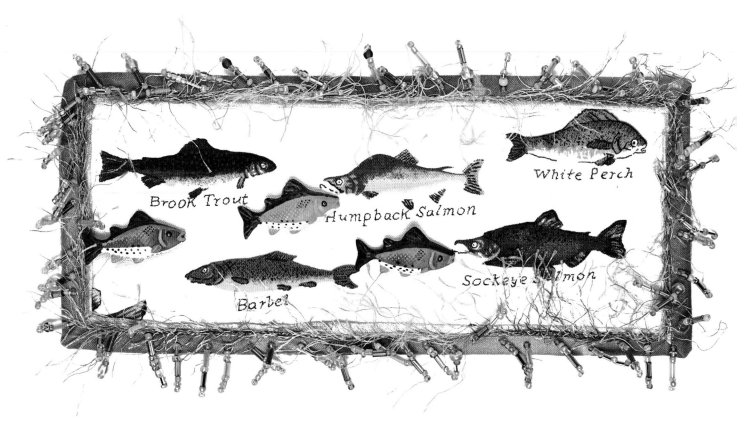

## Fold-Over Binding

Using a zigzag stitch, I added yarn over the top stitching of this super-fast binding and piping edge. Of course I had to add a few beads, too. The sewn-on fish buttons add a nice three-dimensional touch to the printed fabric. 6" x 3"

This is one of the simplest ways to bind your Eye Candy Quilt. The binding and backing fabric are one and the same, so when you choose this method, think about what your finished project will look like when the backing fabric shows on the front. This method has an added advantage when very heavy fringes are added because it provides a lot of support.

**1** Cut the binding/backing about ¾" larger than the Eye Candy to be bound. If the quilt is 2½" x 3½", cut the backing 3¼" x 4¼".

**2** Cut a piece of Steam-a-Seam 2 Lite the same size.

**3** Fuse the two together.

**4** Cut the front fabric and fuse the batting to it with the Steam-a-Seam 2 Lite.

**5** Measure ³⁄₈" from the outer edge and, using a ruler as a straight edge, heavily crease the fabric. Do this for all four sides. The creases will form squares at the corners. With scissors, cut these corners away by carefully snipping along the crease lines. (You will be cutting off a small square-shaped piece at each corner.)

**6** Place the Eye Candy fabric onto the center of the prepared back and check for fit. The folds should fit the front snugly. If they don't, the binding corners will look messy.

**7** Position the folded binding sections over the front and finger press.

**8** When everything, especially the corners, look just right, press.

When the binding is complete, fuse a label to the binding/backing fabric.

This Eye Candy Quilt is bound with a simple fold-over binding. It serves to highlight the large flower and sequins. 2½" x 3½"

# Next Step, Embellishment!

And there you have it—an eye candy blank ready and waiting for you to creatively embellish. With just a little practice, you will be surprised at how quickly and easily you can produce any number of these blank canvases. Since they are a very inexpensive investment in both time and materials, they allow you the freedom to indulge and experiment in every embellishing idea and technique you can imagine.

# Composition— Embellishment Basics!

The fun is about to begin! In this chapter, we begin with a quick review of the best tools for the job of making Eye Candy Quilts, then move quickly on to the basics of creating these little treasures. Once you understand the fundamentals, you will be amazed at how much freedom you have to take your quilt in any direction you choose. And remember, you can change direction any time you please!

## Supply Kit

**Scissors**

**Thread**

**Thimble** (if you use one)

**Needles:** Good choices are #8 or #10 large-eyed "between" quilting needles and #9 sharp "appliqué" needles

**Needle threader**

**Rotary cutter, ruler and mat:** A pinking or wavy edge cutter can be fun

**6" embroidery hoop fitted with a piece of muslin:** I use this to "corral" beads while I'm working because, unlike a plastic holder, the fabric eliminates the static charge that encourages beads to hop out

**Bead scoop:** Useful for pouring beads back into their containers

*Simple tools are all you need to make Eye Candy Quilts.*

# Tools

Most of the tools and supplies you need for making Eye Candy Quilts are already in your sewing kit. You'll need the obvious: scissors (small sharp ones work best), a thimble if you use one (I don't), regular sewing thread, and a needle threader (which will save you time as well as frustration). You will also need a rotary cutter with a blade you are willing to use on paper. A rotary cutter with a pinking or wavy edge blade is best if you have one, and a mat and ruler are definite necessities. Having a bead scoop on hand makes collecting loose beads and pouring them back into containers quick and easy.

When it comes to needles, I prefer #8 or #10 large eye "between" quilting needles because they are easy to thread and the eye fits through the hole of most of the beads I prefer to use. If a longer needle is required to make sewing fringes and dangles easier, I use a #9 appliqué. This is also a good needle to use when you need to thread through very small beads. While useful for jobs like these, the #9 appliqué isn't a favorite of mine because it is hard to thread and I hate the struggle. I don't use beading needles at all because they are very long and flexible, suited only to sew beads to beads, not beads to fabric.

# Fabric, Etc.

Eye Candy Quilts are a delightful way to use small scraps of cherished fabrics, even that "just too precious to use" piece from your stash. When choosing fabric for the front of your quilt, look for something interesting. It might be your favorite color, a fabric you painted yourself, or it could be a scrap that evokes a special memory. Consider using that really weird fabric that just isn't suitable for the quilts you normally make. Textured fabrics work very well, too.

If you are a quilter, you are probably accustomed to using all-cotton fabrics. Well, Eye Candy Quilts give you an opportunity to try something new. They lend themselves easily to virtually any type of fabric, no matter how unusual. A piece of silk from a wedding dress, a bit from an outgrown baby outfit, or perhaps a fun fabric you found at the store and just could not resist bringing home. And, don't forget all those odd little pieces friends may have given you over the years that were just not suitable for quilting.

This quilt started with some pieced fabric with a few small painted leaves. The yellow appliqués were left over from another project and the green flower was purchased. A fused binding and beaded fringe complete the quilt. 2½ " x 3½"

Whatever fabric you select, scraps are all you need; you will not have to shop for new yardage unless you want to. If you decide you want a large background, you can always piece it from scraps. The seams will be covered with embellishment so they won't show.

When choosing fabric, select something for the back of the quilt, too. You will also need scraps of batting and some type of fusible web. I use double-stick Steam-A-Seam 2 Lite. Half the weight of most fusible webs, this brand has a pressure sensitive adhesive that allows for a temporary hold to your materials, so there is no need to press until you are ready.

This project began with a favorite green and white polka-dotted fabric. The binding committed me to a blue and green color scheme so I searched for a large, flat blue bead to serve as the focal point. The white polka dots seemed to lose importance and adding beads around the edges strengthened them visually. By now it had become clear this Eye Candy Quilt was going to be all about circles, so I beaded on more of them. This is a great example of making one decision at a time and letting the design lead you wherever it wants to go. 3½" x 2½"

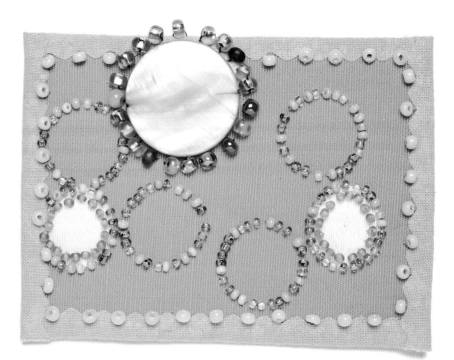

OPPPOSITE: This Eye Candy Quilt is an example of good design. The large purchased green and black sequined appliqué is the focal point. To keep the appliqué from overwhelming the design, the rest of the quilt needed to be equally graphic. I used a multiple-stepped stitch on my sewing machine which was threaded with black embroidery thread. A heavier thread would work too, but I didn't happen to have one on hand. The very large green sequins, called paillettes, and the large black sequins balance the design. 5" x 7"

# Threads for Beading

Beading threads are similar to very thin, long ribbons. The ribbons are made up of strands of fibers, making them strong enough to stand up well to bead edges, which can sometimes be quite sharp. I use and recommend either Nymo (lightly waxed nylon thread) or Silimide (two-ply, twisted, pre-waxed, nylon thread). I prefer to use a color that matches the background fabric. If you don't have access to the rainbow of colors available, I recommend using a medium gray or beige. I use whatever size thread I have in the color I need, as long as it fits through the hole of the bead.

A single strand of Nymo or Silimide beading thread is perfectly adequate for securing most types of smaller beads. If I am attaching a large bead or a found object, I sew through it two or three times for extra security. I've also found that dangles and fringes can take quite a beating (everyone who holds them seems compelled to shake them in order to see them sparkle), so I always double my thread there, too.

Pull on your thread lightly before using it, to prevent knotting. If you prefer, treat it like hand quilting thread and give it an additional coating of wax before sewing.

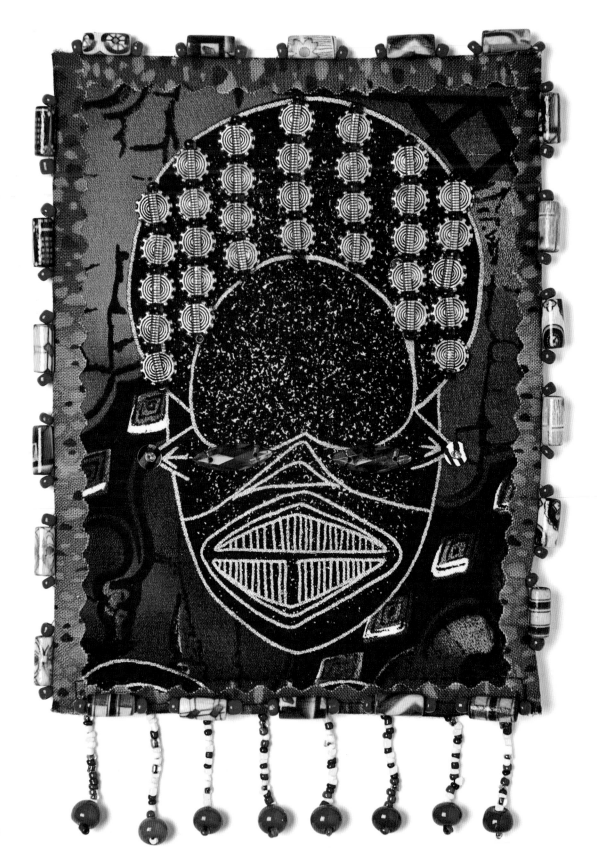

# Design Decisions

Once you begin to think of your Eye Candy Quilts as artistic compositions, you will find this opens the door to all kinds of ideas. Don't let the word "composition" intimidate you. Think of it quite simply as a way of organizing the design elements on your quilt. Before I begin a new Eye Candy Quilt, I take a look at a note posted in my studio. It is a list of simple dos and don'ts that help me keep on track to good design. Here it is.

◆ Avoid distributing the elements of your design in a perfectly symmetrical manner. Variety makes for interest.

◆ Have one main subject or focal point and perhaps one or two smaller items of interest.

◆ Always face the most important design element "inwards" or toward the center of your work. For example, if you have a profile of a person, place the face looking into the center of the quilt, not outwards.

◆ Think about repetition. Repeating shapes or colors is an easy way to make your design effective.

◆ When should you stop embellishing? If you are asking yourself this question, my answer is that you have not yet embellished enough! In my opinion, when you get to the point that it takes 10 minutes to try to find a place to squeeze one last bead into your design, you can be pretty confident you are finally done.

Keep these key points in mind as you work on your Eye Candy Quilts and you will find the work goes more smoothly. They will help you make decisions and solve design problems as you move along.

## Design Symmetry

Symmetrical designs happen when the weight of a composition is evenly distributed. It assumes identical forms on both sides of the center. Asymmetrical balance occurs when the visual weight of a composition is not evenly distributed around the center. It involves the arranging of objects of differing size in a composition so that they balance one another with their respective visual weights. Usually there is one dominant form that is offset by several smaller forms. In general, asymmetrical compositions tend to produce greater visual interest.

OPPOSITE: These decisions were all made one at a time. First I chose the face-pattern fabric. It dictated the finished size. Next came the binding decision—I chose a simple fused binding. I had a wonderful time pawing through my stuff for ethnic-inspired embellishments. I found a scrap of purchased fringe. It only fit across the bottom—no problem! I sewed it on. The bugle-type beads were in my stash, too. I originally wanted to use them as edging, but the thread showed. Instead, I added a small round red bead next to each bugle bead. The gold pieces in the headdress are from a piece of jewelry I took apart, and because red beads had already been used on the edge, I repeated them here. Single black and gold sequins made good earrings. Last, red jewels for the eyes—perfect. By making one decision at a time, I never felt frustrated and love the finished piece! 5" x 7"

This is a good example of asymmetrical design. On the left is a piece of ribbon with squares printed on it. I added a few beads for interest. On the right are oblong shapes of jewelry pieces and sequins. The combination of materials is successful because the shapes are similar. 5" x 7"

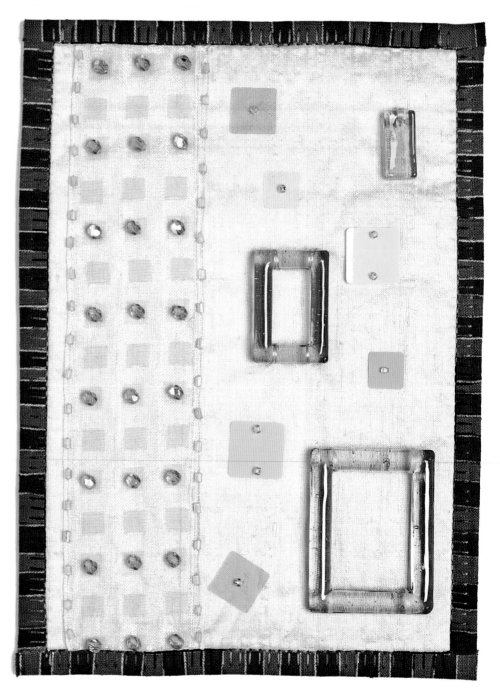

Keeping in mind two rules of composition—the *rule of thirds* and the *rule of odds* will help you better understand symmetry. They will also help you make design decisions for your Eye Candy Quilt.

## Rule of Thirds

The rule of thirds is a compositional tool that makes use of the idea that the most interesting compositions are those in which the primary element is off center. To understand the rule of thirds, visualize a tic-tac-toe grid. Wherever two lines intersect is a good spot to position your focal point. If you divide a picture area into thirds from side to side and top to bottom, then place the subject at the intersection of the imaginary lines at one side or the other, you will often have a more pleasing composition than placing the subject in the center (This is known as the "bull's-eye syndrome" and should be avoided most of the time.) The rule of thirds helps break the bounds of composition symmetry. Asymmetry is much more interesting.

The bee, bee hive, and flower were strategically placed where the lines of a tic-tac-toe grid would meet, following the rule of thirds. Note that the bee hive has no holes, so I attached it with glue. The bugle bead edging does a good job of bringing the background color out to the edge. 2 ½" x 3½"

## Rule of Odds

The rule of odds suggests that odd numbers of elements are much more likely to catch the viewer's eye than even numbers of items. This means that if you have more than one decorative element on your quilt, you should choose an arrangement with at least three of them. An uneven number achieves the desired asymmetry which is more likely to appeal.

The shoes, purse and earrings are the focus here. Notice that even though they are not identical, they still follow the rule of odds. I just could not resist the dress pattern tissue paper in the background—a found object. 4" x 6"

# Focal Point of Design

Have one main subject or focal point and perhaps one or two smaller items of interest. This is another one of those design principals that quilters are aware of but often don't realize they know. One major player with a couple of supporting players is simply more interesting than one embellishment planted dead center. The most attention-grabbing designs draw the viewer's eye to a major item, then smaller items irresistibly lead the eye all the way around the composition, ending back at the main focal point. Thus, the viewer has seen and appreciated all of the parts as well as the whole of your work.

Designs that face out rather than in will appear odd or out of balance to the viewer. It's uncomfortable to look at and leads the eye right out of the picture rather than drawing the viewer more deeply into your work. This is one of those cases that is hard to explain but easy to see, so check out the photo example shown here.

The large button serves as the focal point; the flowers are the supporting players. Since the big button looked a bit stark on its own, I softened its edges with a collar of ruffled trim. 2½" x 3½"

The sailboat is sailing right out of the picture. Looks strange doesn't it? This is an example of an unsuccessful composition. If the sailboat was large and took up the whole space, it would look fine. Or, if the boat was turned around and sailing into the picture, that would also work. 5" x 3"

This quilt combines a variety of embellishments. Beads, ribbon and a ball fringe come together to make a successful Eye Candy Quilt design because they not only have color in common but share the same round shape. The red ribbon printed with turquoise dots provides a nice visual transition from the inside design to the outer edge. This is a good example of the fused frame style: the ball fringe covers the unfinished edge. 10" x 8"

## Repetition

*Repetition* is a fun design element to play with. It happens when objects, shapes, direction, lines, and so on, are repeated in a design. For example, say you have chosen to use a large round button. Adding other round shapes—not just round buttons—will work because they have a shape in common. Think about using round flowers, rings, sequins, and beads both large and small. Or you might repeat a common color, line or texture. The important thing here, again, is repetition. All of these together can add to a design's overall success.

## Knowing When to Stop

How do you know when your Eye Candy Quilt is embellished
enough? Good question, but there is no easy answer. By now you
realize that sometimes I bead until the Eye Candy Quilt is totally
encrusted. Sometimes they are almost sparsely beaded. I look at
each piece as a whole and decide. Over time, my motto has become,
"If I have to ask the question, then the answer is *no*, my quilt is not
embellished enough".

Enough? No question here, this
one is done! 3½" x 2½"

**TOP LEFT:** Eye Candy blank
**TOP RIGHT:** Eye Candy Quilt
partially complete
**BELOW:** The perfect amount
of embellishing. In order for
this large fish to appear to be
swimming into rather than out
of the picture, I backed his tail
up to the far edge. 3½" x 2½"

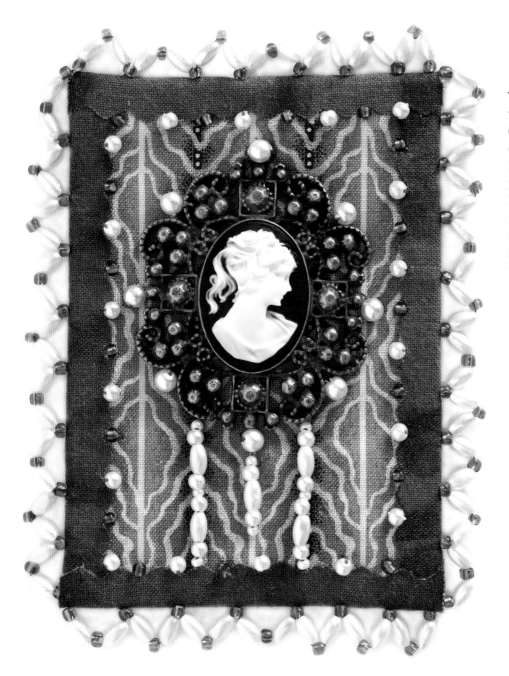

This old fashioned cameo was a purchased pendent. One of the pearls around the edge hides the metal loop. If I had stopped at just one pearl at the top, it would have made my "fix" of the problem blatantly obvious, so I integrated pearls into my overall design and added them all the way around the center piece. The oat-shaped pearl zigzag edging adds just the right touch of elegance to compliment the cameo and make the choice of a pearl camouflage even more natural. 3½" x 2½"

# The Art of Camouflage

Camouflage—or the art of concealment—involves disguising an object in plain sight in order to hide it. I am always aware that what you see isn't necessarily what is really there. It's possible to fool the eye with your choice of bead or other embellishment placement.

Imagine that you have a quilt and the piecing isn't your best. You sew buttons to the centers of each block to hide this flaw. You might want to think about the situation you have created. It's like waving your arms in the air and saying, "I can't piece", and this probably isn't the message you want to send. The viewer knows right away what happened because the buttons are only placed where the errors occur. In this situation, it might be a good idea to scatter lots of buttons around the quilt so they look like a deliberate part of the design. In other words, you have successfully fooled the eye.

Another purpose of camouflage is to draw the viewer's attention away from certain elements so that they focus on other elements. I'm not fond of un-sewing anything, particularly when I have creative ideas flowing freely. Sometimes, rather than undoing any work, I add a new focal point. This helps take attention away from parts of the quilt I don't want the viewer to notice. For example, I might strategically attach a bead in order to firmly secure a binding that did not fuse well.

If there is a particular element of your Eye Candy Quilt that doesn't appeal to you, don't be too quick to rip it out. Instead, take a good look to see if there is a way to cover or tone it down a few notches. You may find that your overall design is all the better for the disguise!

Look at the Eye Candy Quilt in the picture on page 24. It started as green fabric with white polka dots. I sewed on the large blue bead, then beaded around the dots. Looking at the result, I realized that the dots were now far too prominent. So, to tone them down, I added the beaded circles. Now there are many interesting things to look at and the over-domineering dots have become a supporting element, which I much prefer.

# Expectation of Perfection

Let's talk about the expectation of perfection. We all have it to some degree but it can be a real creativity-killer. If your sky-high expectations prevent you from doing what you enjoy or you are ruthlessly critical of your work, where's the fun in that? Instead of demanding perfection from yourself, perhaps you can learn to change your expectations. It is okay if the spacing of your dangles is not absolutely symmetrical. No one will notice, unless you decide to tell them. An Eye Candy Quilt is all about enjoyment—both the making and admiring of it. So just do your best and move on.

Still not good enough for you? Then learn ways to aid yourself without those techniques becoming obvious to the viewer. For example, if you want perfectly even spacing, give yourself some kind of guide to follow. Maybe this is the zigzags in rickrack or the polka dots on a piece of ribbon. Or you might machine stitch around the edges and attach a dangle every fourth or sixth or ninth stitch. Using the "ins and outs" of a binding cut with a pinking rotary cutter is another good aid for spacing success.

My favorite antidote for perfectionism is randomness. My fringes usually have many beads, are often different lengths and the spacing is vastly different. When I change my expectation away from technical perfection to what is artistically pleasing, the goal is much more easily and enjoyably accomplished.

# Beads: What and How

Beads have to be my favorite embellishment. They come in an endless variety of sizes, colors, materials, styles, and sheens that makes my heart pump with excitement.

OPPOSITE: I started out with these round-shaped beaded found objects. To me, they are reminiscent of the twirling skirts you might see on the dancers at a Mexican fiesta, so I needed to find a fabric that was bright and happy. The binding fabric is also red-orange. It frames the quilt without overpowering it. The round, thread-covered hoops are really intended for use as a frame for shi-sha mirrors. I didn't want to add shi-shas because they wouldn't make any sense with my "fiesta skirt" idea, so I put beads in the centers of these hoops, instead. The quilt clearly needed a bead fringe, but nothing that would overwhelm the design. I settled for dangles along the bottom edge and a simpler treatment for the other three sides. 3½" x 2½".

It's fun to spend an hour or two rummaging through a bead store, but if you don't have one in your area, shop by catalog or on websites. The choices are often overwhelming, so you might find it helpful to know what you are looking for before you begin. Study the photos on websites carefully—online looks can sometimes be deceiving. Keep the needs of your project in mind and consider the following guidelines:

- Make a shopping list of what you need—it will help you stay focused.
- Buy only beads that you love—and always buy the beads that catch your eye first.
- Buy more than one size. Variety will add interest to your work.
- It only takes a tablespoon or two of beads to make an Eye Candy Quilt, so go for variety over quantity.

Red, orange, pink, yellow, green, purple, and blue. Beads come in every color of the rainbow, and then some. Shiny or matte; large or small; round, square or oblong, beads are available to please everyone's tastes and designs.

# Types of Beads

Glass is the most common bead material. Glass beads can be either completely transparent or opaque. You may purchase glass beads singly, on strings called "hanks", or in bags, tubes, or other containers. In addition to glass, you can find beads made of bone, wood, and even stone. Metal, brass and aluminum can be stamped into uniquely shaped beads.

Even plastic is a reliable and inexpensive alternative bead material. Whatever you choose, don't get too caught up in all the particulars. Just plan to buy and use beads you love!

Here are a few of the bead types you are likely to come across:

- Seed beads: Small, round, colorful beads, sized by number. The higher the number, the smaller the bead (that is, size 11 is smaller than size 10).

- Bugle beads: Small, tube-shaped glass beads, varying in length from ⅛" to 1 ¼" and available in a wide variety of colors and finishes. Bugles are among the most reflective or sparkly bead types, and they work wonderfully in fringes. Note that the edges can be sharp, so add a seed bead "buffer" at either end of a bugle to avoid cutting the thread.

- **Faceted beads:** The shiniest beads of all, these are available in every color imaginable, in multiple sizes, and in glass, plastic and metal. Their shine is the result of the many facets reflecting light.

- **Drops:** As the name implies, drops are beads that are marvelously shaped in the form of tear drops. The hole is at the top of the drop – the narrow, pointed end. Drops are perfect for making fringes or dangles.

- **Beaded fringe:** Ready-made fringes are a great way to finish an Eye Candy Quilt quickly. Fringes come in a huge variety of sizes, styles, colors and prices. These delectable little treats are irresistible, but tend to be pricy. The beauty of using them on tiny quilts is that an affordable few inches is all you need. When choosing one for your project, think about scale. A 6" long fringe is probably going to overwhelm a 2 ½" x 3 ½" quilt. For this size Eye Candy Quilt, look for lengths that are more in the ½" to 1½" range.

Some beads are not colorfast, so they might flake or fade. To test beads for colorfastness, soak them in water mixed with a few drops of bleach. Rinse well and then dry in a paper towel. If there are small flakes of paint in the towel, the beads are not colorfast. Even though you may never wash your Eye Candy Quilt, non-colorfast beads can still do damage. Over time, they can bleed into or flake all over your work.

To check for fading, compare washed beads against unwashed beads. If the washed beads are noticeably lighter in color, they will definitely fade over time. This method also works well for jewels, pearls, buttons and most found objects.

I purchased the pre-packaged clay flower, lady bug and leaf beads at a craft store. The purple fabric on the diagonal contributed both movement and interest. With the idea of foliage in mind, I added a number of different sizes and shades of green beads and leaves to the background. The border beads are drops, which suggested leaves to me. 2½" x 3½"

A large Asian-inspired bead makes for a very bold focal point. In order to balance the design and give it a feeling of structure, I added red ribbon enhanced with sparkly bugle beads. There are more bugles around the edge to finish it off. Because bugles often have thread-cutting sharp edges, I added tiny seed beads at either end of each one. 5" x 7"

LEFT: Just one of many tubs of beads waiting to find the right Eye Candy Quilt to adorn. Inside the tubs, my beads are sorted into individual film canisters and plastic bags. Notice the film canister with the bit of green ribbon. This designates the "scraps", meaning leftover beads that were mixed together during the creation of a previous project. It would be a tedious task to separate each bead back into its original container, so I always plan to use the mix—as is—on another project

# Bead Placement

Choosing where beads are to be placed is strictly a personal design choice. I look to the fabric to "speak" to me. Sometimes there will be a design in it I particularly want to highlight or something I want to play down. I happen to like the action of sewing beads to the surface, so sometimes I sew them on just because it's fun. Beads can be used to attach appliqués, buttons, sequins, ribbon or any other type of trim. Sometimes the dangle spacing just doesn't look quite right, so I add a spacer bead or two, as needed. This is especially helpful when I am going around an outside edge corner. This is also a useful technique to hide the bale on a jewelry pendant. Here are some general guidelines for bead placement.

ABOVE: The metal cabinet in my office houses beads as well as many other embellishments. Almost everything is stored in see-through plastic tubs, arranged by color and type, and labeled on both ends. Remember to store your treasures in a cool, dry place.

- Plaid or check fabrics: try placing beads at the intersections or in the centers.
- Scatter beads over all or part of the surface.
- Affix beads onto buttons or appliqués.
- Use beads to fasten ribbon or other trim.
- Beads can be sewn in peaks or valleys of a decorative binding.
- Use beads to attach sequins.
- Use beads to attach silk flowers.

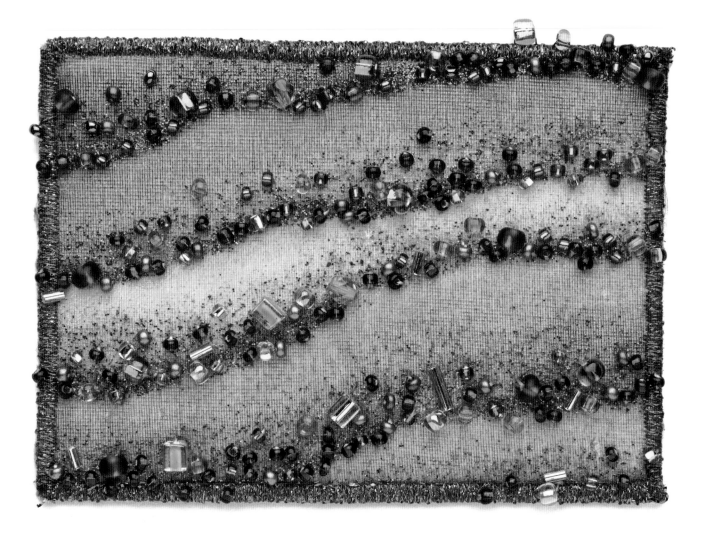

A colorful ribbon is fused to a solid-colored background fabric and finished with a thread binding. The placement of these beads is dictated by the design of the background. Happily, the ribbon has sparkly flecks of color; matching my bead choices to the flecks lends a subtle depth to the design. To me, the overall effect is reminiscent of the wave action on a sandy beach. 3½" x 2½"

Remember, too, that beads can be a camouflager's best friend—use them to hide your mistakes!

Most of my beading is done with a variety of beads. This look appeals to me and is easy to achieve. I purchase beads that I like and, because I know in advance that I will undoubtedly mix a number of different beads together, I never need worry about buying an exact number of any one bead.

When I'm ready to start sewing, I gather a collection of beads together that I think I might like to use and pour some of each out onto my fabric-lined embroidery hoop. With my needle, I line a bunch up in a row and sew them on in that order, which I call 'streaming'. Since I've already decided the beads look good together, I don't need to stop my sewing in order to decide exactly which bead will be placed in what spot. If I run out of one of the selection, I can ignore it, choose to add a different bead, or go to the store and buy more!

# Attaching Beads

If you are new to embellishing your quilts, you'll find that beads at first are tricky and slippery to work with. Still, with a little practice and patience, you will be handling them like an expert. These guidelines should help. Approach beading as you would embroidery. I work as much as possible from the front face of my project; I try to keep the work tidy and professional-looking and to not sew through to the back, as this looks sloppy to me. Instead, I slip my needle between the layers.

## Securing Basics

1. Thread a needle with a single strand of Nymo or Silimide thread; make a quilters' knot.

2. Start about ½" away from the first bead location, and pull to "pop" the knot (i.e., pull it between the layers), coming up in the quilt next to where the first bead is to be placed.

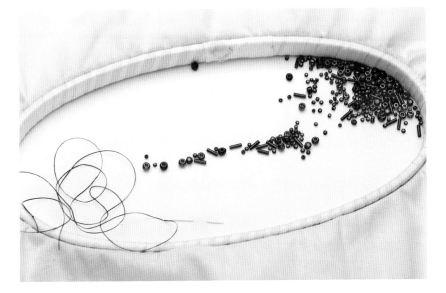

To make the decision process easier, I use my needle to line up some beads. This dictates the sewing order. I call this "streaming."

3 Place the bead on the needle and insert it into the fabric next to the bead. The stitch needs to be just as long as the bead, but no longer (or the thread will show too much).

4 Continue until you come to the end of the thread and end as you would for a line of hand quilting, securing the end by again "popping" the knot.

ABOVE: Beads are used to fasten the ribbons into place on this fused frame. The bright pink faceted beads around the edges are secured with locking beads of a complimentary but slightly contrasting color. 4" x 6"

OPPOSITE: I pulled some small silk flowers off the stems. Beads served the dual purpose of becoming the flower centers and fastening them securely into place. I added one matching bead to the butterfly, just so the major features would look like they belonged together. 2 ½" x 3 ½"

> **Tip** *I find it is safer to take a second stitch through every third or fourth bead. This serves as a "knot". If the thread should happen to break, two or three beads will come off, not the whole group. I recommend running the thread through larger, heavier beads three or four times.*

# Running Stitch

The running stitch is a simple way to attach beads on one at a time. To sew the beads, bring your needle up through the fabric from the wrong side about ½" away from where you want to place the first bead and "pop" the knot. Then place the needle into the bead's hole and slide it onto the needle with the tip of your finger. Insert the needle back into the fabric on the other side of the bead and come up where you want the next bead to be placed. The size of the stitch should be slightly smaller than the bead so the thread doesn't show, but not so tight that it distorts. Pull the thread firmly. This is the simplest way to sew beads--one at a time.

# Backstitch

The backstitch has a couple of uses. It can be used to stitch one bead at a time when very close spacing is desired. You can sew several beads in one backstitch. When sewing a group of beads, you need to come back up under the second or third bead from the end and go through that bead and the rest and come out the last bead. Then pick up another group of three to six beads (I have the best success with four), line them up, and repeat. This is the backstitch. It secures the line of beads so they won't move. The most important skill to develop is to be able to sew on the beads in a way that secures them in the proper position and stabilizes them. For example; you can have the first stitch lay down six beads. The next stitch came up behind the fourth bead and goes through beads 4, 5, and 6. Next, add the next group of beads, laying them down either in a random fashion or along a pattern line. Secure them with a down stitch, then backtrack again, so that most of the beads are stabilized with double stitches.

Running stitch

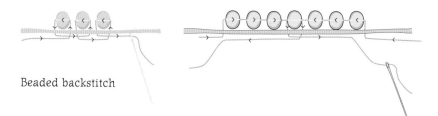

Beaded backstitch

Sometimes it's all about the fabric, or rather what's printed on it. This Eye Candy Quilt is my memory of Paris. I printed my photograph on prepared-for-printing fabric. Since I had it in the back of my mind that Paris is known as "The City of Light", I wanted to use a variety of sparkly beads rather than some other trim to balance the very strong vertical line of the Eiffel Tower. I very densely beaded the two (asymmetrical!) columns using a back stitch, utilizing masking tape guides to keep the lines straight. 2½" x 3½"

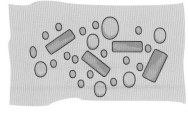

Scattered and dense bead spacing

## Attaching Scattered Beads

I like the look of a variety of beads sewn on in a random fashion. Sometimes there is a reason for their placement, often not. Using the running stitch for sewing the beads onto the surface, I can make the spacing appear reasonably even by using the length of the needle to measure. Sometimes I scatter beads quite closely. This look takes dedication and works best when a variety of shades, sizes and shapes of beads are used. It's much harder to scatter in a random pattern than you would think. Your brain will often try to impose order, even when you don't want it to! Watch your work closely for unintentional patterns or lines, which can easily creep in to disrupt your desired randomness.

When attaching ribbons, I scoot the ribbon with the tip of the needle and add a bead in the scattered format. Sometimes there are lots of beads, sometimes not. Either way works beautifully.

## Beading in Straight and Curved Lines

Keeping the lines of beads perfectly straight can be challenging. To make them line up like soldiers, sew the beads on one at a time using the running stitch or in groups of three or four with the backstitch. If the beads are very small, this is one time I make sure to use thin thread. After the line is sewn, go back through all the beads with one single thread. I prefer to use a small diameter, longer appliqué needle for this purpose. If the bead line is too long for the needle, come out when necessary, pull the thread through and continue with the needle through the bead tunnel to the end. The only time it is necessary to pierce the fabric is at the beginning and end.

To make a curved beaded line, sew the beads in the basic manner (small,

First thread

Straighten and strengthen lines of beading. This is best done with a small appliqué needle and small thread.

Second thread

single strand of thread) until your line of beads is the desired length, making the stitches in a curved line. Always make corrections to accommodate the curve when the needle comes up. To force the curved line of beads to be smooth, bring a new thread up from the back side of the fabric just underneath the last bead. Enter the "tunnel" of beads, and exit when it becomes difficult to travel further. Do not stitch into the fabric, but continue through the tunnel. Keep going until you reach the end of the line. Give the thread a slight tug and the beads will adjust themselves perfectly into the curve you are trying to achieve.

## Attaching "Locking" Beads

Use this technique to "lock" one bead or embellishment in place with another bead. Sequins, charms, trinkets and buttons can all be attached in this way.

1. Begin by popping the knot, then string one large bead onto the thread.

2. Follow the large bead with a smaller bead, remembering that the smaller bead must be larger than the hole of the large bead.

3. Pass the needle back through the hole of the large bead, going around the outside of the small bead.

4. Pull the thread completely through to the wrong side of the fabric and secure.

Locking beads

# Beaded Edges

Beaded edges provide a spectacular opportunity to focus on beads. A very attractive edge can be as easy as sewing on one bead at a time all the way around an Eye Candy Quilt or attaching many beads strung on thread. The variations are endless. Beaded edges can be very elaborate; these are usually made up of dangles and fringes. Dangles are a single strand of beads. Fringes are composed of a series of bead strands (dangles) that create a decorative border. Both of these styles inevitably require the use of a locking bead. Fringes and dangles are great fun to sew and just wonderful to look at. I'll show you some and invite you to see what else you can create on your own. The potential variations are absolutely limitless.

Not all beaded edges need to be either fringes or dangles. These single seed beads were stitched one at a time to the edge making an informal frame for the center design. 3½" x 2½"

- **One bead edging.** Stitch one bead at a time along the edge until you have gone all the way around your Eye Candy Quilt.

- **Stacked two bead edging.** Slip a larger bead on the thread, then a second, smaller, locking bead, skip your needle around the outside of the locking bead on the return but back through the larger one. Slip your thread into the fabric and come up where you want the next one to be and repeat all the way around.

- **Bugle bead edge.** This edge consists of single bugle beads sewn around the Eye Candy Quilt. I generally use single seed beads at either end of bugle beads to prevent the sharp-edged bugles from fraying the thread. The single seed beads also help facilitate even spacing.

- **Picot.** Slip three beads on your thread and make a backstitch only one bead long. This forces the beads to "stack," creating the picot.

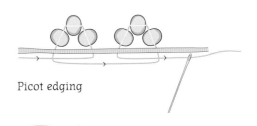

Picot edging

It's always nice when you can draw your viewer's eye into the middle of your Eye Candy Quilt, then out to the edge, and back to the center. The more interesting people find something, the longer they look at it and vice versa. The shiny bugle beads around the edge are a subtle but effective way of accomplishing this. 3½" x 2½"

What a difference this easy
picot edge makes! 2½" x 3½"

# Dangles and Fringes

Pre-made fringes can be attached either by machine or hand stitching. Your might also want to fuse them on. Steam-A-Seam 2 Lite comes in ¼" and ½" precut strips all ready to use. Add some to the back of the edging, finger press into place, and iron.

The shiny looped trim and silver border seemed to just beg for a series of dangles. These are a combination of shiny bugles and multiple sizes of seed beads. 2½" x 3½"

Although it is a bit more trouble, I usually hand-make my own dangles and fringes using a double thread. There is something intensely satisfying about creating my own original fringe. The thread seems to want to tangle, but the dangles are much more secure. Dangles can go all the way around an Eye Candy Quilt if that fits with your design, but also look great when sewn to just one side. This side nearly always, just because of the nature of dangles, seems to visually become the 'bottom' of the mini-quilt, but you can flip it over if that suits your artistic eye better.

1  To begin a fringe, double your thread. Pull the needle and thread out of the fabric and "pop" the knot. Add a series of beads to make up the first strand. Add the locking bead.

2  Take the needle around the locking bead and back through all of the rest.

3  Continue until the fringe is the desired width.

4  Pull the thread completely through to the back side of the fabric and secure.

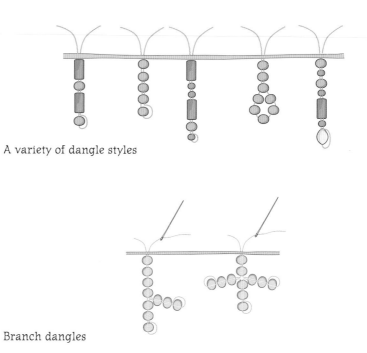

A variety of dangle styles

Branch dangles

A branch dangle is a very effective variation. It allows you to include lots more beads, too! Make a small stitch and string beads onto your thread to the desired length. Pass the needle around the outside of the locking bead and push it back through part of the beads on the string. Add more beads to your thread, again skip around the new locking bead, and pass your needle through the rest of the beads on your original string. Make a stitch and continue to the next dangle.

This full dangle border combines a variety of beads. I selected the beads I wanted to use, put them in my fabric hoop corral and sewed them on in a random fashion, sticking out this way and that, which seemed to suit the feathery yarn trim very well. I like the variety and it is easy to sew.  3½" x 2½"

## Scalloped Edges

Make a small stitch at the edge of your project, pick up seven beads and make another small stitch. Return the needle through the first two beads. Pick up five more beads, make a small stitch. Continue around the quilt. When you stitch around a corner, add a few more beads as necessary in order to keep the beaded edging flat.

Scallops

OPPOSITE PAGE: Start with a favorite fabric, in this case I chose a pink and green batik, then look for other embellishments that might work well with it. Using the pink, green and a little gold ribbon for extra interest, I needed something to attach the ribbons, so beads came next. I then decided to add fringe and secured it with a blanket stitch using hand-dyed pearl cotton, then stitched on an olive green fused frame. 5" x 7"

LEFT: It's perfectly okay to let the border take on star status, too. This Eye Candy Quilt's simple but effective center allows the double looping fringe to shine. 3" x 3½"

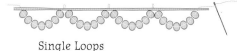

Single Loops

## Single Loops

An informal looping of beads makes a graceful pattern. The sewing is simple; just make sure you use the right thread. To loop, make a stitch and slide the beads onto some doubled Nymo thread. Put your needle back into the fabric at the end of the desired loop, make a small back stitch, add more beads and continue on.

## Double Loops

Go around your Eye Candy Quilt first, making one single loop. Then go around again, making the second loop by making a stitch in and out again about halfway into each of your first set of loops. Add more beads and continue on.

Double Loops

## Zigzag Edges

Zigzags are very successful when sewn with long or oval beads. You will need both a long variety and some seed beads. To zigzag, make a stitch, alternate one seed bead, one long bead, one seed bead, one long bead, one seed bead onto your doubled Nymo thread. Take a very small stitch in the binding about ¼" away, come up through the last seed bead, and repeat as needed.

Zig Zags

# Special Embellishments with Beads

There are a number of special effects you can use to enhance your beads. Here are just a few ideas to get you started.

## Beading Covered Buttons

Use either a pre-manufactured covered button, or a covered button blank which can be found at any fabric store, and cover it with your chosen fabric in the way the package directs you. Pop your initial knot, sew on your beads, buttons, sequins, etc., and finish up by popping the last knot.

# Three-Dimensional Beaded Shapes

Three-dimensional shapes are fun and easy to make. It's simple to liven them up by just changing the sizes, shapes and colors of the beads you choose. I am giving directions for a dragonfly here, but don't overlook other shapes such as flowers, butterflies or bees. You might also try circles or squares. A variety of bead sizes and shapes works very well for 3-D shapes. Be sure to choose the wire that fits through your beads at least twice. The pliers are necessary to bend and shape wires and to pull the wire ends through the beads. Cutters make it easy to trim the ends. To make the dragonfly, follow these steps.

This elegant design started with the beautiful pink covered button in the center. It was a bonus that the manufacturer had already covered it. Since I happen to like lime green and pink together and found the pinkish-green ribbon, an Eye Candy Quilt was born. I attached beads to all of the buttons, both singly and in dangles. The large leaves are from the craft store, the small shiny leaves started out as sequins of some other shape that I cut into the leaf shapes you see. A few beads here and there assure the binding will stick and also secure the ribbon in place. 4" x 7"

## Dragonfly Body

This sparkly three-dimensional dragonfly perched upon an Eye Candy Quilt makes a cheerful picture. 3½" x 2½"

1   Cut a 6" piece of .014" fine stainless steel/nylon coated wire and fold in half.

2   Slide a medium bead onto the wire.

3   Slide a ½" bugle bead over both wire ends.

4   Slide another medium bead followed by another long bead, medium bead, tear drop bead, medium bead, and larger round bead for the head.

5   For the antennae; separate the two wires and slide short bugle beads onto each wire. Using pliers, fold the ends of the wire back into the bugle beads.

6   Trim wire ends as necessary.

## Large Top Wings

**7** Cut 17" of .014" fine stainless steel/nylon coated wire.

**8** Slide four medium beads onto the wire followed by one long bugle bead, repeat.

**9** Add one medium bead (different than the others), one bugle bead (again different), then another medium bead.

**10** Slide one long bugle bead, four medium beads, repeat (these should be the same beads as step 8).

**11** Slide both wire ends through the crimp tube.

**12** Repeat steps 7-10 for the second large wing. Slide both ends of the wire through the crimp tube.

## Small Bottom Wings

**13** Slide one long bugle bead, three medium beads, then one long bugle bead onto the wire.

**14** Add one short bugle bead, one medium bead, then one short bugle bead.

**15** Repeat step 13.

**16** Slide wire ends through crimp tube and into the first long bugle bead. Leave some slack in the wire.

**17** Squeeze the crimp tube with the pliers and trim any excess wire.

Sew the two pieces onto your Eye Candy Quilt, making sure the body is on top of all four wings.

### Supplies for 3D Dragonfly

- .014" fine stainless steel/ nylon coated wire (very small wire good for small diameter beads with round edges)

- Round-nosed pliers

- Wire cutters

- Crimp tubes (available at craft stores, these are small round tubes that can be squeezed using pliers to hold the wires together)

- Beads—both bugle and round beads

The wings are made in the shape of two figure 8s, one smaller than the other.

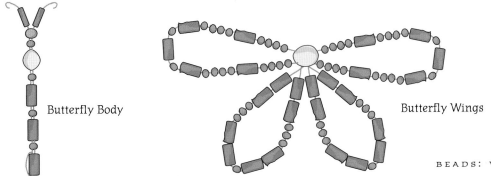

Butterfly Body

Butterfly Wings

# Baubles and More!

Beyond beads, there is an endless variety of materials at your fingertips to embellish your quilts. As you will discover, when in comes to Eye Candy Quilts, anything goes! Once you open your eyes to the possibilities, you will find new ideas for embellishments everywhere you look.

**OPPOSITE:** It's all about the jewels! The pink flower jewel along with the butterfly set the mood to create a flower garden. A smattering of jewel centers, stitched leaves and petals were all that was needed to finish. 7" x 5"

# Jewels, Pearls, Sequins and Shi-Sha Mirrors

Jewels, pearls, sequins, and shi-sha mirrors add a wonderful variety of shape, texture, color and shine to any Eye Candy Quilt.

## Jewels

Jewels have flat backs and a mirror finish, giving them lots of sparkle. They are easy to find at your local craft store. Be sure to notice that some come with pre-drilled holes for sewing, and some are sold without holes, intended for use with glue. No one will know if you glued down your jewels – unless you tell them!

## Pearls

Pearls always add a touch of elegance. White is not the only color option – you can find pearls in several pastel shades including blue, gray, pink, ivory, champagne, green and lavender. Most often, pearls are sold pre-strung or pre-packaged with holes drilled through the center, making them as easy to work with as beads. They look great when you mix and match them with beads or other embellishments.

This purchased appliqué with a single pearl at its center caught my eye as a perfect Eye Candy Quilt embellishment. To complement the center pearl, I put oat pearls (oblong shaped pearls) with tiny coral-colored seed beads around the quilt border, and then added pearl dangles along the bottom of the design. The appliqué itself is so big and bold that the basket-weave fabric chosen to support it all but disappeared. While I normally prefer to scatter beads, this is one occasion where the quilt itself demanded pearls be placed at regular intersections in the fabric. 7" x 5"

## Sequins

Sequins come in more shapes, finishes, sizes and colors than I can possibly list. They may be flat, cupped or square, transparent, iridescent or opaque, stars, ovals or circles. Sequins are available in virtually any color and come either loose or on strings, generally sized from 3 mm to 50 mm. Their variety is glorious. Sequins can be sewn on without using beads. Just come up through the hole and down over an edge. Do this two or three times, spacing out your threads. I like the extra shine that sequins contribute and prefer to not cover any of it up, so I usually sew mine on with beads. A bead locks each sequin in place. Bring your needle up the through the fabric then through the hole in the sequin and the bead. Pass it around the bead, and then back through the hole in the sequin and into the fabric. Then either knot your thread or move on to the next sequin/bead combination.

The soft blue background fabric inspired me to pair it with an iridescent lamé binding, which acts as a subtle border. Star sequins explode across the quilt, all the way to and beyond the edges, in an exuberance that matches the night sky. Notice the stars are attached with three different textures of round sequins as well as beads. 5" x 7"

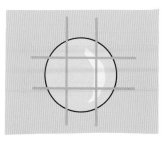

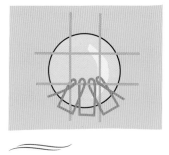

How to attach shi-sha mirrors

## Shi-sha mirrors

Shi-sha mirrors are available in a variety of materials from mica flakes to glass and plastic. Traditional shi-shas are round, but you can also find triangles, squares and other shapes. They are generally available in sizes from ½" to 1 ¼".

Even though there are no holes in a shi-sha to pull thread through, there is an easy method for sewing them onto a quilt. Begin by sewing a tic-tac-toe grid over the shi-sha. Next, embroider over it by bringing your needle up through the fabric at the edge of the shi-sha, looping it through the grid, and gently pulling the center square of your tic-tac-toe design back just a bit to form a frame around the glass. Push your needle back through the fabric. Continue all the way around until the shi-sha is firmly held in place. The photo here shows the result.

These shi-sha mirrors were attached with pearl cotton, using the method sketched out here. 2½" x 3½"

## Paillettes

Paillettes are an alternative to shi-shas, without the sharp edges. They are large sequins; usually with a hole near one edge. Whereas shi-sha mirrors are available only in a finish that looks like a mirror or a rainbow mirror, paillettes come in a variety of colors, sizes and finishes, ranging from transparent to iridescent, satin (matte) to opaque, as well as metallic and holographic.

## Buttons

Whether you are lucky enough to have salvaged your grandmother's button box or you shop for buttons, these little beauties make for great embellishments. Made from precious metals, bone, porcelain or workaday plastic, buttons come in a virtually limitless array of colors, shapes and sizes. Be sure to check both sides of your buttons—the backs are often as interesting as the fronts!

Buttons take the lead role in this production. Two gold buttons are surrounded by gold rings with different textures for more interest. A large red button is covered with a purchased appliqué. The beads on this button are there simply to cover up the thread in an attractive way. Since this is a straight, rather than wavy, binding edge it needed a bit of machine stitching to hold it in place. 3½" x 2½"

Experiment freely with the way you sew buttons onto your Eye Candy Quilts. Remember that these buttons are strictly decorative, not functional, so the urge to sew only through the center holes is an irrelevant restriction. Consider sewing your buttons on with a different color thread, or use more than one thread color on the same button. Try stacking buttons on top of each other and sewing them on that way. You might also try sewing from the center hole to the edge, as you would sew a sequin. Try different threads, too. For instance, attach the button with a thick thread and either knot or tie a bow right on top! Need a particular color? You can always change a white button by coloring its entire face or just part of it with a permanent marker. Of course, you can also add beads to buttons or hang dangles from the center holes—the possibilities are endless.

Shank buttons—those with a plastic or metal shank for sewing rather than center holes—are a little problematic on Eye Candy Quilts because they don't lie flat. One way to address this and stop shank buttons from wobbling is to add a "collar" to stabilize them. A collar is simply a piece of ribbon or other trim, hand stitched on one edge and gathered to form a circle, like a slightly ruffled collar. If a collar doesn't work with your overall design, place a few beads under the button to support it.

**ABOVE:** Buttons and lace seem to make a natural pairing. Here, I wanted the lace to tuck under the binding but the fusing wasn't strong enough to hold it. I solved the problem by machine-stitching the binding down and, at that point, buttons turned out to be just the right thing to add. Embellishments don't have to match exactly as long as there is some unifying element. Here, the buttons are all round and coordinate with the colors of the background fabric. 2½" x 3½"

**RIGHT:** Each button is sewn on using a different method. Clockwise from the upper right: Sewn from the center to the outer edge of the button; beads sewn through the center holes; attached using beaded dangles; sewn with French knots; attached with bead; embellished with a trim collar. 3½" x 2½"

# Decorative Threads

Decorative threads, such as embroidery floss, pearl cotton or sewing machine thread in whatever color that works for your project can add a wonderful texture to Eye Candy Quilts.

Six-strand cotton embroidery floss is the thread most commonly used for hand embroidery. It's inexpensive and available just about everywhere. It's even available in metallic finishes. Usually sold six-ply, the threads can be divided or left intact, depending on your design requirements. Pearl cotton is available in four sizes and comes in many colors. Metallic pearl cotton, a twisted, metallic thread, is available in size 5 only. Neither of the pearl cottons can be divided.

Don't overlook the possibilities of machine stitching threads. There are now some wonderful thicker threads made for machine quilting that are perfect for hand-sewing as well. Variegated threads produce the effect of ever-changing thread color, achieved in the easiest possible way.

Dress up almost any button by sewing it on with a contrasting color thread. Tie it on with pearl cotton or use a piece of ribbon to stabilize a shank button. 3½" x 2½"

# Ribbons, Rickrack, and Lace

Textured fabrics like ribbons, rickrack, and lace can bring interest and excitement to your Eye Candy Quilts. You can also use them to blend nicely with your background fabrics, allowing other embellishments to shine!

## Ribbons

Gleaming, soft, rich, beautiful and happy are just a few of the words I associate with ribbon. Ribbon is one of my favorite materials to play with on Eye Candy Quilts. I like to use picot-edged ribbons, partly because they make positioning other embellishments a snap. The little looped edges are evenly spaced so placing a bead, a fringe or a dangle in every loop makes the spacing right every time. Small ribbons with regularly spaced polka dots are another easy way to evenly space beads.

When you have strong design elements, such as this blue flower and terra cotta-colored flower pot, you need to be sure your supporting players don't completely disappear into the background. This quilt would not be the same without the six-strand embroidery floss stems and grass. They add an important integration to the overall design. The border of bugle and larger round beads adds a balancing bit of texture. 2 ½" x 3 ½"

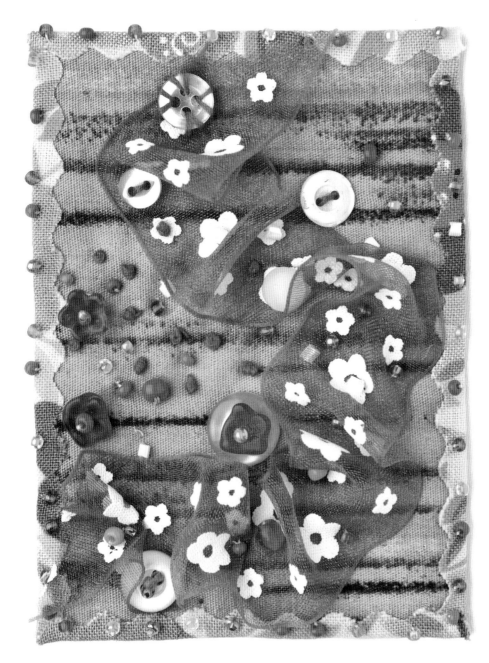

This joyful Eye Candy Quilt is all about the ribbon. I purchased sheer orange ribbon pre-printed with flowers. I love sheer ribbon, since it can be scrunched into any shape I please. When it is flat against a matching-colored fabric you may not notice that the ribbon is there, but scrunch it together and it shows up well. It's very easy to scoot the ribbon with the tip of a needle and secure it with beads, buttons or stitching. 2 ½" x 3 ½"

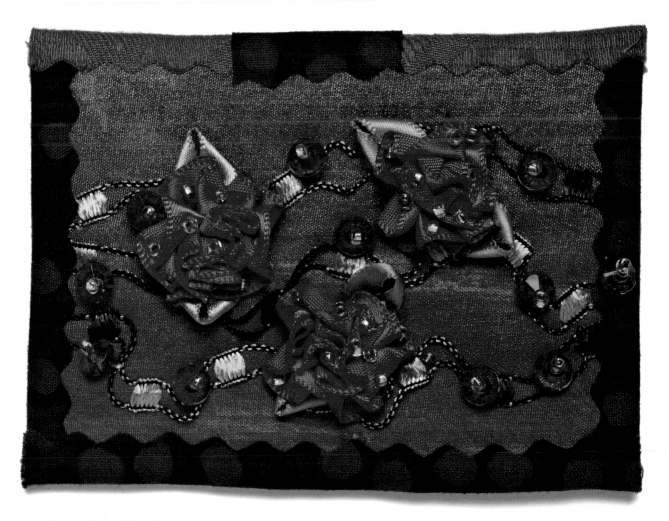

My favorite color happens to be red and a few purchased ribbon roses make this Eye Candy Quilt really pop. I added the trim because it suggests rose trellises. The beads on the flowers are like dew glistening in the sun. 3½" x 2½"

With ribbons and other trims, I recommend testing for colorfastness. Wash a small piece and blot it with a paper towel. If the towel stays white, the trim is unlikely to bleed and you can go on your merry way. If you are still unsure and need to pre-wash the whole piece of trim, launder it just like delicate fabric, putting the pieces in a mesh bag before tossing them in the machine set on its "delicate" cycle.

Ribbons and other trims are a great way to add a lavish look to your Eye Candy Quilt. Look over your stash and find a scrap or two of ribbon that will work well with your project. Ribbons, like any other fabric, are happiest when kept dust-free and away from light. I store mine in an untidy heap in plastic tubs because I enjoy rummaging through them, constantly rediscovering old favorites or finding new ones. All it takes is the right piece of ribbon to inspire me and I'm off to my next Eye Candy Quilt project.

# Rickrack

Rickrack is surely the boldest of trims. It comes in three sizes; the small and medium widths are perfect to use on Eye Candy Quilts. (The largest rickrack size would likely be a bit overwhelming to this mini-medium.) Rickrack is available in cotton and polyester in a wide selection of colors. It is perfect for these tiny quilts because it can be hand or machine sewn on an edge and the peaks or valleys can be utilized for exact bead or other embellishment spacing.

**ABOVE:** The first thing most people see are the sequins, which, you will notice, are a variety of sizes and textures. Now take a second look at the rickrack trim. It came from the store with the beads already attached, making it a super-easy addition and it is bold and bright enough to hold its own in the overall design. 4" x 5"

**LEFT:** The rickrack used here is very showy. To make it even more important, I highlighted the points with beads. The orange appliqué and yellow button were purchased; the yellow appliqué is one I stitched myself. 2½" x 3½"

## Lace

Lace is easy to find on old clothing, pillow shams and many other places. You can buy it as easily as trim. I often purchase lace yardage, both expensive and cheap, depending on what I fall in love with. When placed over solid-colored fabric, lace adds great texture. Lace is available in a variety of fibers, colors and styles. It just takes a scrap or two to embellish an Eye Candy Quilt. Lace trims can be cut into decorative motifs and many of them can be colored with fabric paint or even permanent markers. What a wonderful way to commemorate a wedding with a special bit of wedding lace!

**ABOVE:** The center section is a piece of lace-like ribbon. Of course, the bonus was that the beads were already attached. I added lace pieces to both sides to make the lace more prominent. The picot beaded edging echoes the lace edges. 2½" x 3½"

**RIGHT:** An Eye Candy Quilt can have multiple elements. Pink lace placed over the tissue lamé started this extravagant design. On the top and bottom I added two purchased trims enhanced with pearls. The item in the center is a treasure from the bottom of my button box. I think it's a yarn-covered button – but maybe not. It doesn't really matter, does it? After all, part of what makes Eye Candy Quilts so much fun is the treasure hunt experienced when I visit my stash of embellishment goodies. I added a pearl button to the center and a few beads to the yarn. The edging is alternating purple beads and pearls. 2½" x 3½"

# Found Objects

Found objects are perhaps one of my favorite types of embellishments. They can include a huge variety of stuff. Old jewelry purchased at a thrift store or garage sale, an odd appliqué, buttons that seem too large, especially those without shanks, can all find a happy and permanent home adorning an Eye Candy Quilt. When you look around, you will see materials everywhere that, while they have little or no use in traditional quilting, can make an Eye Candy Quilt amazing. Walk up and down the aisles at your favorite craft store and see what you can discover. Be receptive to the voice in you that says, "That's interesting".

In the found objects category, I include items originally intended for some other purpose. Jewelry findings are the best example. Gold and silver rings (meaning shapes – not for fingers) and pendants are, forgive the pun, gold mines. We all seem to have a bag of broken jewelry. These are great items to adorn Eye Candy Quilts. I use a pair of pliers to remove the usable pieces and then discard the rest. If you happen to lose a favorite earring, you can display the other by featuring it in its own Eye Candy Quilt. Or perhaps you have a pin you never wear, or silk flowers or an odd piece of beaded fringe. Think about belt buckles, scrap-booking supplies, paper clips, safety pins, whatever can be re-purposed. Remember, anything goes! That's what this book is all about.

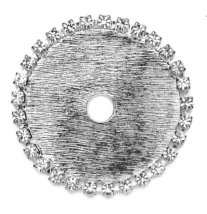

Found objects—what is this thing? I have no idea, but I found it and loved it. How could I possibly pass up a round gold piece bordered with sparkly faux diamonds?

The black fleur-de-lis shapes were iron-on embellishments purchased at a fabric store. The jewelry-making section of my local craft store was the source of the silver rings and the silver zigzags are leftover bits of fusible bindings. I saved the best for last...the silver rings at the bottom are fancy paper clips adorned with a few beads. 7" x 5"

**RIGHT:** Symmetry isn't always a bad thing. The square jewelry trinkets just insisted on being arranged in a pattern. I added red sew-on jewels because they repeat the color and shape of the trinket centers. The quilt looked unfinished, so I added red beads along the edge. 4" x 7"

**ABOVE:** Scrap-booking supplies made it easy to add a message to this Eye Candy Quilt. I purchased the words and chose a background fabric that would highlight them. Oat pearls added just the right touch of elegance. This is an example of a traditional style binding, which I embellished with cross-locked craft beads. 7" x 5"

An unidentifiable object has found a home. At the right of the quilt is a bead with a gold ring around it (sewn on with nearly invisible Nymo thread). The middle decoration is a pin I found with a slightly larger gold circle added around it. My unidentified "found" treasure supports a special button and surrounds it with jewels. Not only do the sparkles look great, they cover up the uninteresting part of the object. Notice that repeating the circular motif makes the whole Eye Candy Quilt look unified. 7" x 5"

The background fabric is hand-painted in red with gold highlights for extra interest. The leaves are two pieces of fabric fused together and cut into leaf shapes. To add dimension, the flower centers are all large beads held in place with locking beads. The overall cheerfulness of this little Eye Candy Quilt inspired the pink beaded edge. 3½" x 2½"

# Play and Display

Now that you know how fun, fast, and easy it is to make Eye Candy Quilts, it's time to celebrate them—on the go, on display, or at a party. It takes just moments to make up your own Eye Candy kits to take with you on vacation, retreats, or anywhere you have just a little time to play.

OPPOSITE: This green Eye Candy Quilt combines found objects and various beads from a kit I prepared in advance. 2½" x 3½"

The creative rewards are enormous. And once you are addicted to making these sweet little treats, you will want to display them all, so check out some of the ideas presented in this chapter. Use any or all of them and create some of your own display ideas.

Everybody loves a party! Invite friends over to tap into their creative abilities by making Eye Candy Quilts together. Just a little bit of preparation will make your party the one everybody remembers.

# Make Eye Candy Quilts On the Go!

Eye Candy Quilts are perfect "make-on-the-run" projects. If you commute to work, travel on business, or spend time in doctor's offices or at kids' activities, you need something to keep your hands busy. It is easy to make up a kit for your next Eye Candy Quilt and have it at the ready to take with you on your next retreat or vacation, or to work on during lunch time! What a wonderful way to enjoy quilting and make the best use of all those moments in the day when you are on the run but not really occupied.

To make up an Eye Candy Quilt kit, all you need start with is a gallon size plastic zip lock bag filled with a few supplies. In my "necessity bag" I always include a pinking rotary cutter, mat and ruler, plenty of my favorite Steam-A-Seam 2 Lite fusible web, needles, a color assortment of Nymo threads, small pieces of batting, my embroidery hoop fitted with muslin, and my favorite small scissors. Sometimes I make a few eye candy blanks (see page 7) at home where it is easier, but this isn't really necessary if there is an iron at your destination. To make up kits for myself, I choose things just because I happen to like them. Start with a piece of front fabric and a pre-labeled back. Add a binding material unless you are using the fold-over binding

Eye Candy Quilts are small enough to be made anywhere. I assembled this variety of supplies to take with me on vacation. A word of caution – I have found that often my fellow travelers become so enamored with these small creations that they want to make one of their own.

method described on page 18, which doesn't need anything but a slightly oversized backing piece. If you are planning on a separate binding, it might be the same fabric as the front, or, because jazzier is sometimes better, you might choose a binding that highly contrasts with the front fabric, making it an additional design element. The key in all of this is choosing something you like right at that moment.

My kits often include many possible embellishments that might or might not be used. I look for buttons, beads, sequins and found objects. I use anything that catches my eye that I think will work with the front fabric. Most of my Eye Candy Quilts have a focal point. This might be a special bead or button. Appliqués, whether hand-made or purchased, are good focal points. I also pack at least two supporting players or more if I might want to make up my mind about which to use once work on the Eye Candy Quilt is actually underway. For example, I might find two buttons that would be perfect to highlight that one special appliqué, or I might bring a small container full of optional buttons. How wonderful that everything is so small and easy to pack!

Ribbon adds great texture, so I might toss in some bits of these as well. If the pieces of ribbon are very short, it's often a good idea to bring many of them. Why not include wide, narrow, sheer and shiny ribbons in your kit? They can be intertwined and secured with beads.

Because beads are my favorite embellishment, I usually bring more than will ultimately be needed. Fortunately, they are extremely small and I don't have to make very many hard choices about what to leave behind. I like to make beaded fringes using a variety of different shapes and colors, so I choose what to take accordingly. If the front has a strong color I might bring anywhere from two to four tablespoons of different beads that are the same color with one or two that are different. A variety of sizes, colors and textures not only looks great, it's much easier to work with because you never have to worry about running out of any particular type of bead while you are away from home, which would be very inconvenient. There are packages of assorted beads out there just waiting for you to purchase. Personally, I buy lots of them!

If there is a sewing machine available at my destination (there often are at quilting retreats), I might include some thread for machine stitching the edges or making thread bindings. If I have a special trim or yarn to couch around the edges, I pop them into my kit as well.

And, if there is a town, shopping center or even just a fabric or craft store nearby, remember you can always decide to yield to the temptation of going treasure hunting for more goodies for your Eye Candy Quilt.

This Mexico-inspired Eye Candy Quilt really pops when hung from a fancy rod. And it's not really all that fancy; just a ¼" acrylic rod, 20 gauge wire and a few beads. 3½" x 2½" (This rod was actually free—I did a quick internet search of "plastic rods" and found a local display stand maker who cheerfully raided his scrap bin and gave me all the rods I wanted.)

# Display Your Work

There are nearly as many ways to display Eye Candy Quilts as there are Eye Candy Quilts to make. You can pin one or several together on a decorative ribbon; show one off on a miniature easel; attach Eye Candy Quilts to picture frames with a pin or sticky-backed hook and loop dots. Try one of the many methods described here, and soon everyone who sees your work will want to make Eye Candy Quilts of their own!

# Decorative Rod Hanger

To embellish a simple acrylic rod hanger so that it showcases your Eye Candy Quilt, you will need a few things from your stash or the craft store as listed here.

String a few beads on the wire and wrap it around the dowel or rod. Force all the beads to face the front and manipulate the coils into a pleasing arrangement. To craft the hooks, cut two pieces of wire about 3" long. Using pliers, bend the wire into a heart shape, with the cut at the "cleavage." It's easier to get both pieces the same size if you bend them both at the same time. Sew the point of the heart to the Eye Candy Quilt and attach the hooks to the rod. Gorgeous!

Making a beaded wire rod is easy. I wrap a piece of string or yarn around the rod or dowel to estimate how long a piece of wire I will need, and then cut the wire. Use needle nosed pliers and bend down the tip of one end of the wire. Select beads in a color or colors that compliment your Eye Candy Quilt and string the beads onto the wire. Once you have strung the beads, clip off any extra wire leaving just enough to bend over the ends so the beads can't slip off. Now all you do is wrap the wire into a tight spiral around a pen or pencil.

# Beaded Hook

Make a beading hook like the ones used to hold decorations onto Christmas trees—just one more way to display your Eye Candy Quilts.

You'll be surprised how quick and easy these hooks are to make. Clip about four inches of wire. A small thread spool makes a perfect template for winding the top part of the wire into a hook shape. Bend the wire counter-clockwise to make the hook then, on the straight end, thread on a very pretty bead or two. When you thread on the last bead, bend the

## Supplies for Hangers

- ◆ Painted dowel or acrylic rod, in proportion to the size of your quilt
- ◆ Beading wire in a color suited to your quilt
- ◆ A few beads with center holes large enough to fit over the wire
- ◆ Wire cutters
- ◆ Round nosed pliers

## Supplies for Beaded Hook

- ◆ 18 gauge copper wire or similar wire that you have on hand
- ◆ Assorted pretty beads
- ◆ Needle nosed pliers
- ◆ Large and small thread spools to bend the wire around

This quilt started when the fancy trim caught my eye. Since the trim is so visually strong, this Eye Candy Quilt needed other elements that could hold their own with it. I painted the green-checked fabric and decided the butterflies, found in my supplies, were just the right color. Orange seed beads playfully defined the flight path of the butterflies and I also added beads to the border. The quilt looked finished but I was still in the mood to add more beads. What to do? Make a fancy beaded hook to hang it on! 2½" x 3½" wire slightly so that the beads won't fall off. Around a larger thread spool, bend a large loop, again going counter-clockwise. Sew the larger loop to your Eye Candy Quilt for this novel way to display your work. A fun option would be to string beads onto the wire to spell out a name or special word.

This piece of wire was given to me by a student in one of my classes. I thought it made a perfect hanger for this Eye Candy Quilt. Its addition made the whole thing look like an adorable (if somewhat over-the-top) purse. 5" x 4"

## Other Display Ideas

A decorative frame makes a nice Eye Candy Quilt presentation. Cover the mat inside it with a piece of batting and then fabric. A pretty piece of paper, the kind often used for scrap booking, would work well too. Attach the quilt with a straight pin or apply a dot of sticky-backed hook and loop tape to both the Eye Candy Quilt and the frame.

A small easel is one of the simplest ways to display your Eye Candy Quilt. They may be purchased at a craft store. Find one that enhances the style of your mini-quilt and discover the joys of instant gratification. So easy to rotate your quilts too!

A plate holder is an easy way to display your work. 4" x 6"

This simple easel, purchased at a craft store, makes changing your Eye Candy Quilt display a breeze. 3½" x 2½"

Just have minutes available to whip up a project? Using a fused blank, some appliqués with fusible web added and a fused piece of beaded trim made this no-sew Eye Candy Quilt a project that was finished in no time. 5" x 7".

Ribbon is an eye-catching way to display Eye Candy Quilts. I chose black grosgrain ribbon and folded over the top. Adding a black button created a little extra interest. Then it was just a matter of straight pinning the Eye Candy Quilt to the ribbon. For additional security, these quilts can also be attached with safety pins. 3½" x 2½"

I purchased this small heart shaped frame with the intention of turning it into a bit of Eye Candy art. 4" x 4"

The black and white presentation elevates this Eye Candy Quilt to art status. It is simply done with a black document frame, a piece of white paper and a couple of pins. 5" x 7"

A fused blank, some stickers and a fused piece of beaded trim were all it took to make this no-sew Eye Candy Quilt. It's a quick, easy and personalized bon voyage gift for a friend. This style also makes a great rainy-day project for children. 3" x 5"

## Party Supplies

For no-sew Eye Candy Quilts, you will need a supply of scissors, fusible web, irons and ironing surfaces, and fabric glue for everyone. You don't necessarily have to already own enough of everything; ask guests to bring some things along, such as scissors and irons, to share. You will also need a few rotary cutters, rulers and mats (pinking or wavy edge cutters, too). A 6" embroidery hoop fitted with a piece of muslin for each guest is a necessity in order for them to be able to "corral" their beads while working with them.

If you and your guests are going to sew your Eye Candy Quilts, make sure you have a good supply of needles and Nymo thread.

# Let's Have a Party!

Everyone loves a party! Invite your friends and celebrate a bridal shower, birthday, girls' night out—or just because it's Tuesday. Any excuse will do, if it gets your group together to ignite each other's creativity.

The steps to prepare for hosting an Eye Candy Quilt party can be as simple or as elaborate as you like. Start by deciding how much time you want to dedicate to making these very special little quilts. If you only have an hour or your friends don't sew, you will probably want to make no-sew Eye Candy Quilts. On the other hand, if you have two or more hours, sew away!

## Make Eye Candy Blanks Ahead of Time

Sew or no-sew, you will need plenty of eye candy blanks for your guests (see page 7). Decide whether you want to make them in advance or if you will let your friends make their own. Decide, too, whether the blanks will be all the same size and fabric, or if you want to give your guests a variety of blanks to choose from. If you decide to make blanks in advance, be sure to have more than one per guest, just in case you have an extra friend or two show up. And, in nearly every crowd, there is at least one super-fast person who will finish one Eye Candy Quilt and want to start on a second.

There are a number of good reasons to make identical Eye Candy Quilt blanks for everyone. Imagine how special a wedding shower would be if each guest made their own commemorative Eye Candy Quilt to either keep or give to the bride? If everyone starts with the same blank, the quilts will forever remind each guest of the occasion. You might have wedding-themed embellishments on hand, such as material similar to the bridal gown and/or bridesmaid's dresses, scraps of wedding lace, and so on. To celebrate a special birthday, a new baby, a graduation, or other special event, have a few appropriate-themed embellishments on hand and let your guests surprise themselves at how unique each person's creation turns out to be, despite the identical blanks.

## Making the Blanks

Choose the quilt top fabric. To make a batch of ten blanks, you will need a piece of fabric 27" x 37". Cut fusible web, batting, and backing to the same size, layer the pieces together and fuse. Cut into 2 ½" x 3 ½" blanks.

The next step is the binding. The easiest and fastest way to make each binding the same is to cut a piece of binding fabric and a piece of Steam-A-Seam 2 Lite to 13" x 15" and fuse them together. Cut the binding pieces and fuse to all sides of the Eye Candy Quilt blanks. (See page 9 for more detailed directions.)

## Show Guests How to Make Their Own Blanks

To allow guests to make a variety of Eye Candy blanks, have a selection of pre-cut front fabric pieces available to choose from. It speeds things along if you precut the fusible web and batting pieces. Plan on your guests utilizing the fold-over binding technique described on page 18, as this requires the fewest supplies. The instructions are easy, too. Remember you will need several irons and ironing surfaces on hand for your guests to use for fusing their Eye Candy Quilts.

## Share Embellishments

If you wish, you can supply all the embellishments your guests need, but I think it's more fun to have everyone bring beads, buttons, lace, or other decorative items of their own. Still, to make sure you have enough to go around, plan on having the following for each guest:

- ◆ One focal point: button, larger bead, appliqué, silk flower, found object, or other embellishment.
- ◆ Two supporting players (can be different than the main focal point): buttons, special beads, appliqués, found objects, or other decorative items.
- ◆ One to three small pieces of ribbon, trim, lace, and so on, in matching or contrasting colors.
- ◆ Various sequins, jewels, and the like.

Guests who choose to sew will also need two or three tablespoons of beads each to make into dangles and fringes. Remember to vary the size, shape and color for a more interesting Eye Candy Quilt. Non-sewers will need about 14" of pre-made beaded fringe or other trim and might enjoy trying out a variety of stickers, such as those used by scrap bookers.

## Pre-Make Kits for Everyone

If you and your friends enjoy a creative challenge, make up a kit for each guest before the party. This is especially fun if you can scrounge a bunch of found objects. It's hilarious when someone finds they have a bunch of paper clips or an unidentifiable "thing" to work with. The trading and bargaining becomes fast and furious when people see an item in someone else's kit that they covet for their own Eye Candy Quilt.

Making Eye Candy Quilts can be a wonderful excuse to get together with your friends. What can be more fun than to plan an evening's escape and invite your favorite people along?

### Fast and Easy

For gatherings with friends or fast fun with children, keep the non-sewer in mind. Choose one of the fusing methods described on page 9 and look out for embellishments that work best without sewing. There are fusible appliqués available for purchase or you can add fusible web to the back of an appliqué you already have. Stickers from the scrap booking section of the craft store are another option. Look for glue-on beads or other fast and easy embellishments, too.

# Also by Melody Crust

Making a quilt is sometimes like baking a cake—all the fun is in the frosting! In *Quilt Toppings*, Melody Crust offers hundreds of ideas for embellishing quilts, showing that the fun doesn't have to stop after the quilt top is done. From paint techniques to crayons and fabrics, from beading to buttons and bows, and from thread play to the sheer joy of stitching, this book covers it all. Each chapter includes an Idea Gallery featuring dozens of photos of sensational quilt toppings.

- ◆ Hundreds of color photos, with close-up detail of embellishment techniques

- ◆ Before-and-after shots, transforming plain quilts into extraordinary works of art

- ◆ Exciting resource for technique and inspiration

ISBN: 0-9781-933308-02-9 $29.95

Available from Breckling Press 283 Michigan St., Elmhurst, Illinois 60126
www.brecklingpress.com

800 951 7836 (630 941 1179)